THE INN KEEPER OF BETHLEHEM

THE INN KEEPER OF BETHLEHEM

Nick Della Valle

ELM HILL

A Division of
HarperCollins Christian Publishing

www.elmhillbooks.com

The Inn Keeper of Bethlehem

Published in Nashville, Tennessee, by Elm Hill, an imprint of Thomas Nelson. Elm Hill and Thomas Nelson are registered trademarks of HarperCollins Christian Publishing, Inc.

Elm Hill titles may be purchased in bulk for educational, business, fund-raising, or sales promotional use. For information, please e-mail SpecialMarkets@ThomasNelson.com.

Publisher's Note: This novel is a work of fiction. Names, characters, places, and incidents are either products of the author's imagination or used fictitiously. All characters are fictional, and any similarity to people living or dead is purely coincidental.

Library of Congress Cataloging-in-Publication Data

Library of Congress Control Number: 2019910266

ISBN 978-1-400326884 (Paperback)
ISBN 978-1-400326891 (Hardbound)
ISBN 978-1-400326907 (eBook)

Each year, at this time, we gather to share in the telling of the birth of Jesus Christ, The Son of God.

I didn't know. How was I supposed to know? Nobody told me.

My name is Tekoa. I am the inn keeper of Bethlehem.
The one who turned away the Son of God.

That whole week was most unusual. Our little town of
Bethlehem had travelers and people all through the city.
You would've thought it was the Holy City of Jerusalem itself!

That night, it was well after the supper hour when a very weary traveler and his pregnant wife arrived, seeking refuge from the night's chill.

Well, there was no room for them or anyone else for that matter. That night, all my rooms were full!

So, I led them out behind the inn and we walked down the
road and across the field until we got to the stable area where
I kept couple goats and lambs
and one scrawny donkey.

As we laid down, she closed her eyes and, of course she went right to sleep!

I tossed and turned. I couldn't get to sleep at all
and it was because of that light!

I opened the shutters and there, on the hillside faraway in the distance,
was a glorious light! The sky was ablaze with angels!
And they were dancing about and they were singing
to the shepherds as they tended their sheep!

Glory to God.

...on Earth

Peace

&

Good Will Toward MEN

on Whom God's favor Rests

Peace on earth.

So, I laid down and I fell into a wondrous sleep.

I heard the sound of travelers and the hoofbeats
of either horses or camels. They were very near!

Then I got to the front door of the inn and I listened through
the crack to see if I could hear anything outside.

I opened my door to take a peek outside and there before
me, were three splendid riders! They looked to be Kings!
They were seated upon the largest and most magnificent
camels I have ever seen!

As I watched them go down the road, I was preparing to follow them and then…they turned! In the direction of my stable! Did they know where they were going?

I moved closer to see what was going on.

It was then when I noticed that Joseph had stood up and he had greeted the kings. I heard them say they had come to see the child and so Joseph gestured toward Mary and the baby.

She now placed the baby in the manger; it was full of straw.
Then, each one of the kings went over to that child and, one by
one, they got on their knees and they worshipped this child!
Kings!... On their *knees!*

The first king came before the child and gave him the gift of GOLD.
(Was this child a king?)

Then the second visitor came and he placed in front of the child the gift of frankincense.
(Was this child a priest?)

And the third king, he brought the most mysterious gift of all—the gift of myrrh.
(Was this child a healer? Or was he destined for an early grave?)

Gold, Frankincense, Myrrh

It was then when I noticed the star traveling across the sky.
It was the biggest and brightest star I had ever seen
and it seemed to stop and hover over the manger area.
Then the tail of the star came down and, I swear to you,
it lit up that child as if he glowed.

And it was then when I remembered the words of ancient scriptures.

Now I know—this is The One! This is the child I had heard about my whole life.
My heart was full of happiness; my eyes were full of tears;
but my mouth was empty of words. The One I had hoped for had arrived!

Oh! And of all the places in all the world where he could have been born!
He was born in my stable! Wait till I tell my friends! The Son of God …

The Son of God … was born in … my … stable.

Oh, my friends, I tell you, I didn't know. I didn't know!
What have I done?

No one had told me but I'm telling you this night, this Jesus is the Anointed One: He is the Only Begotten Son of God; He is the Christ. And, this night, He stands and He knocks at the door of your heart. Don't turn Him away. Don't push Him away like I did! Open up your mind, open up your heart, open up your life. Invite Him in!

Jesus is the Key!

It was on that starlit night of long ago when the inn keeper of Bethlehem earned the undesired distinction of becoming the first person to turn Christ away; yet, he was not turned away by God, for the Father sent his Son for all people.

+++++++++++++

CPSIA information can be obtained
at www.ICGtesting.com
Printed in the USA
LVHW102020301019
635894LV00002B/2/P